THE

BAD

DAY

BOOK

Swan Huntley is a writer and illustrator living in Los Angeles. Her novels include *Getting Clean With Stevie Green*, *The Goddesses*, *We Could Be Beautiful* and *I Want You More* (2024). She earned her MFA at Columbia University and has received fellowships from MacDowell and Yaddo.

THE BAD DAY BOOK

SWAN HUNTLEY

PENGUIN LIFE

AN IMPRINT OF

PENGUIN BOOKS

PENGUIN LIFE

UK | USA | Canada | Ireland | Australia
India | New Zealand | South Africa

Penguin Life is part of the Penguin Random House group of companies
whose addresses can be found at global.penguinrandomhouse.com.

First published in the United States of America as
The Bad Mood Book by TarcherPerigee, an imprint
of Penguin Random House LLC 2023
First published in Great Britain as *The Bad
Day Book* by Penguin Life 2023
001

Printed and bound in Great Britain by Clays Ltd, Elcograf S.p.A.

The authorized representative in the EEA is Penguin Random House
Ireland, Morrison Chambers, 32 Nassau Street, Dublin D02 YH68

A CIP catalogue record for this book is available
from the British Library

ISBN: 978-0-241-65373-9

www.greenpenguin.co.uk

MIX
Paper | Supporting
responsible forestry
FSC® C018179

Penguin Random House is committed to a
sustainable future for our business, our readers
and our planet. This book is made from Forest
Stewardship Council® certified paper.

This book is for you
and all your future bad moods

Hey, UK friends!

A quick clarifying note before we begin:

This book frequently repeats the term 'bad mood', which might cause you to be like, 'Excuse me, I thought we were talking about my bad *day*, not my bad mood.'

If this bothers you, you can blame me. I originally called this great work of art *The Bad Mood Book*. Then your fellow Brits at Penguin Random House UK made the excellent point that some people might feel judged by that title. I think it's because a bad mood may seem like your fault whereas a bad day seems like the fault of the day.

The real point of this note is to say that I'm not judging you. In fact, all the palm trees of Los Angeles and I are sending you love.

Swan

Hi.

I'm sorry
you're in a
bad mood.

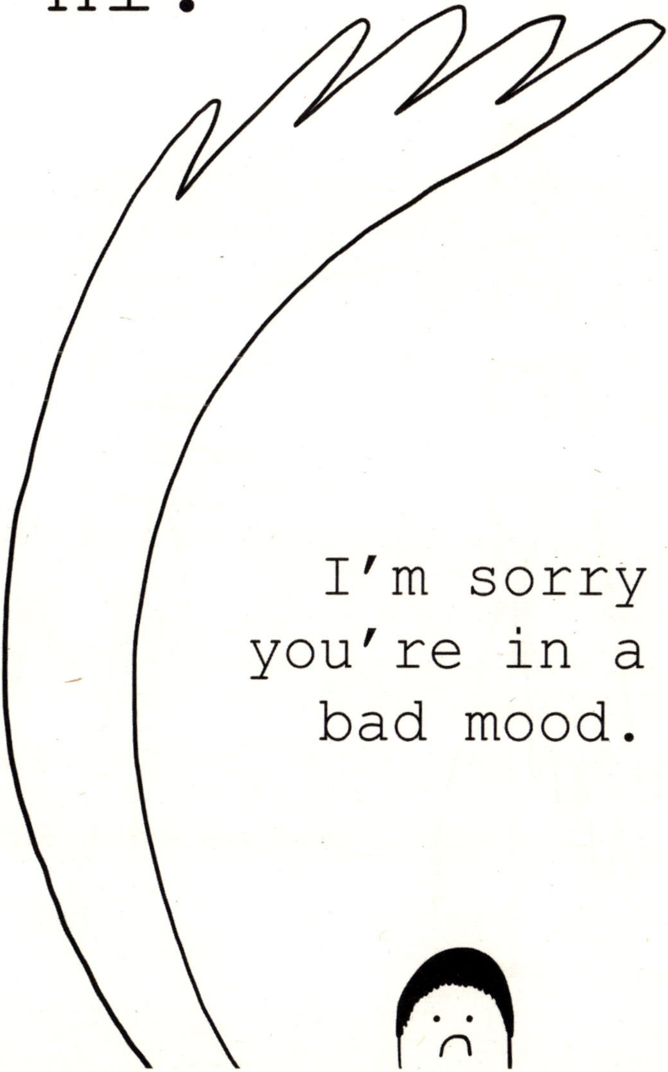

This is me putting my
arm around you.

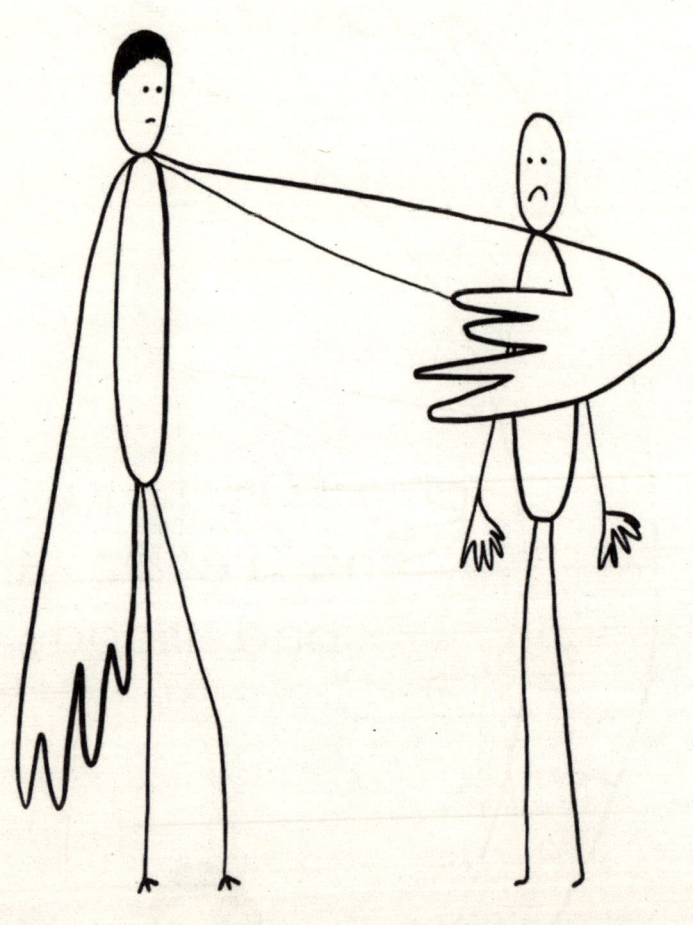

Can you feel the warmth
on your back?

☐ Yes
☐ No
☐ Fuck off

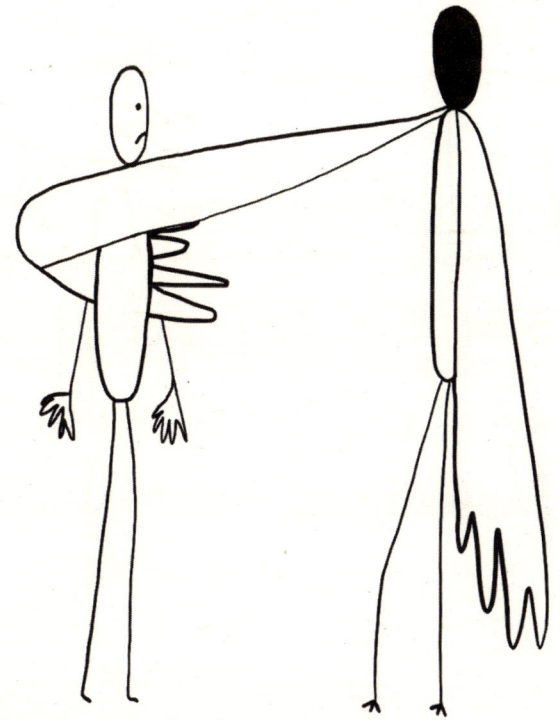

A bad mood
compromises
the
imagination,
so if you
answered "no"
or "fuck off,"
that makes
sense to me.

If your bad
mood is anger-
flavored,
please punch
this dot.

●

If it's
sadness-
flavored, you
can cry onto
the dot.

●

A bad mood
compromises
the ability to
see the humor
in life, so if
you didn't
find that
funny, that
makes sense to
me.

Before we
continue,
let's define
the goal of
this book.

The goal of
this book is
not for you to
viciously
grasp at a
good mood.

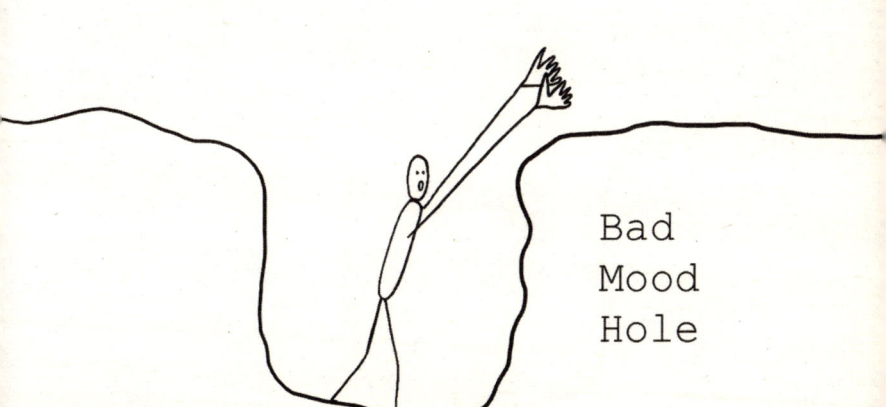

Bad
Mood
Hole

The goal is to
curl up in
your Bad Mood
Hole and ask
some
questions.

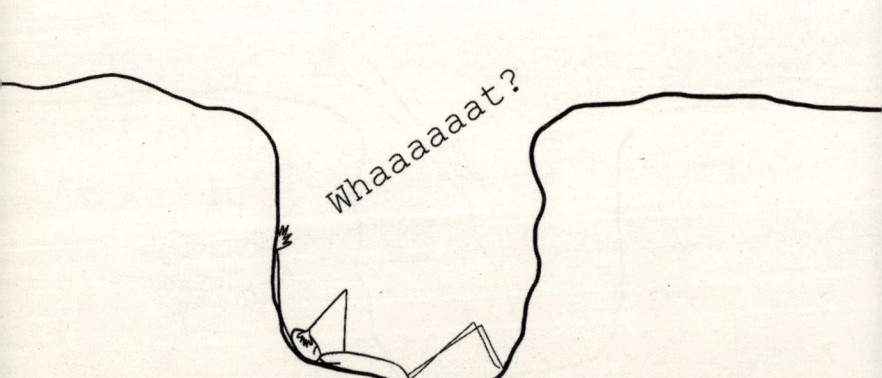

So, please tell me, why are you in a bad mood?

Is there anything else?

The reason I
ask is because
there's always
something
else.

Mostly, when we're asked why we're in a bad mood, we give a local reason. In other words: a reason about something that is happening in our small world.

For instance:

Work is hard.

People are hard.

Having a body is so inconvenient.

But beyond our small world there is The World, and there are lots of reasons to be in a bad mood about The World.

For instance:

People are starving.

People kill other people.

The icebergs are on fire.

Basically,
your bad mood
is a fried
egg.

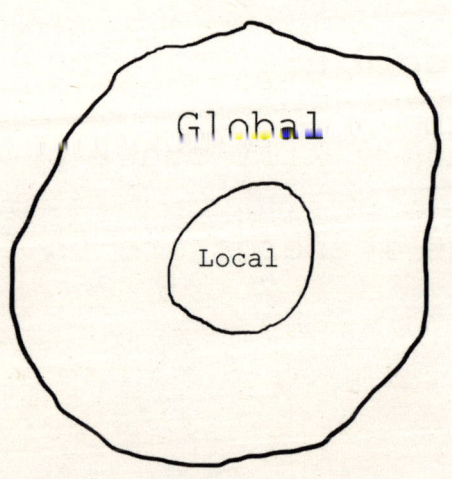

So, can you think of any other reasons why you might be in a bad mood right now?

Another way to
consider your bad mood
is as a layered cake—
with the fried egg on
top.

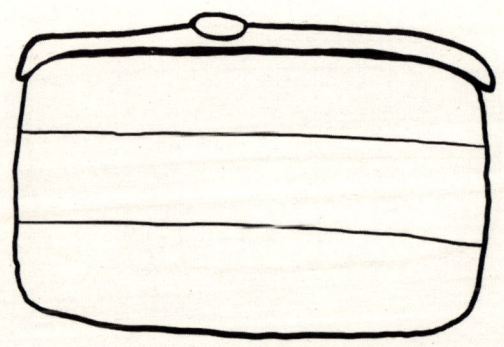

The local and the
global reasons are the
surface of your bad
mood.

Underneath that, there
is what your bad mood
means about you.

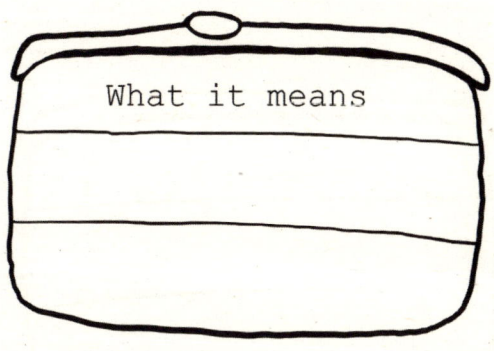

What it means

Usually, the meaning
we attach to a bad
mood is pretty low-
vibe.

What do you think your bad mood means about you?

You know how sometimes when people are in a bad mood they resort to just making sounds?

For instance:

Ugggghhh!

Aaaaaaaah!

Faaaaaaa...

That's because below
the meaning you've
attached to your bad
mood, there's a deeper
layer of historical
reference.

This layer is filled
with primal sadness
and cannot be
expressed in words.

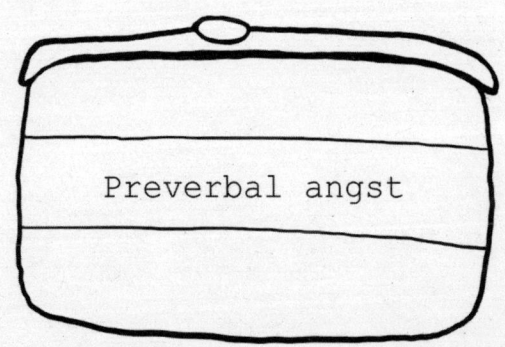

Preverbal angst

Since language is useless in this no-language territory, please draw what your bad mood feels like to even if you suck at drawing.

Last up is...

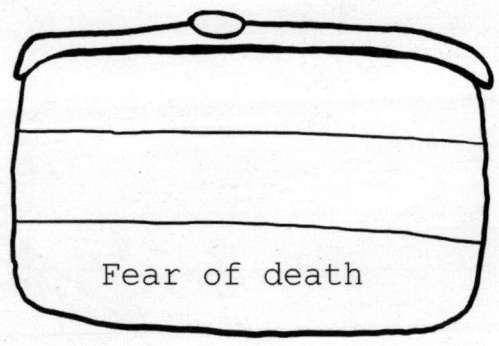

Fear of death

I'm sorry, but it always boils down to this.

I know.

Death.

So final.

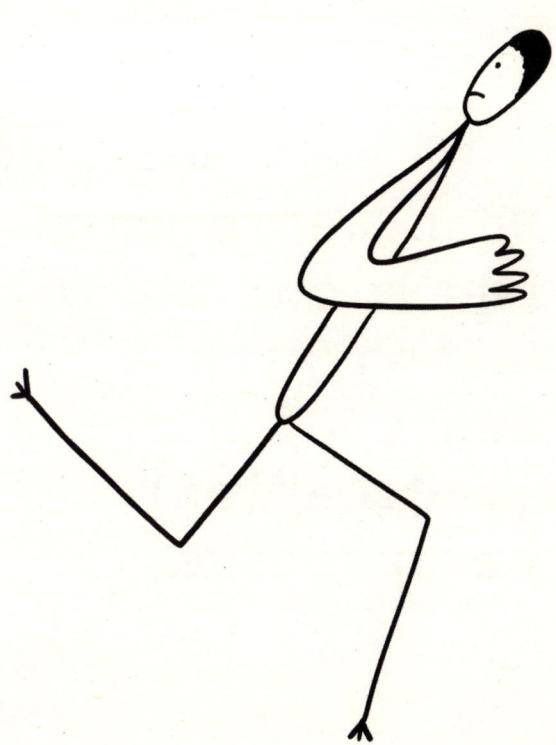

But the upside of
pondering death is
that it gives us a
sense of
perspective.

When we're in a
bad mood, we lose
(along with a
sense of humor and
imagination)
perspective.

In Bhutan, Asia's happiest country, there's a saying about how in order to be a truly happy person, one must contemplate death five times daily.

Let's ignore the specific five times
thing and write this on every line:
I am going to die one day.

_____

_____

_____

_____

_____

_____

_____

_____

_____

_____

_____

_____

_____

_____

_____

_____

_____

This is me putting my arm
around you again.

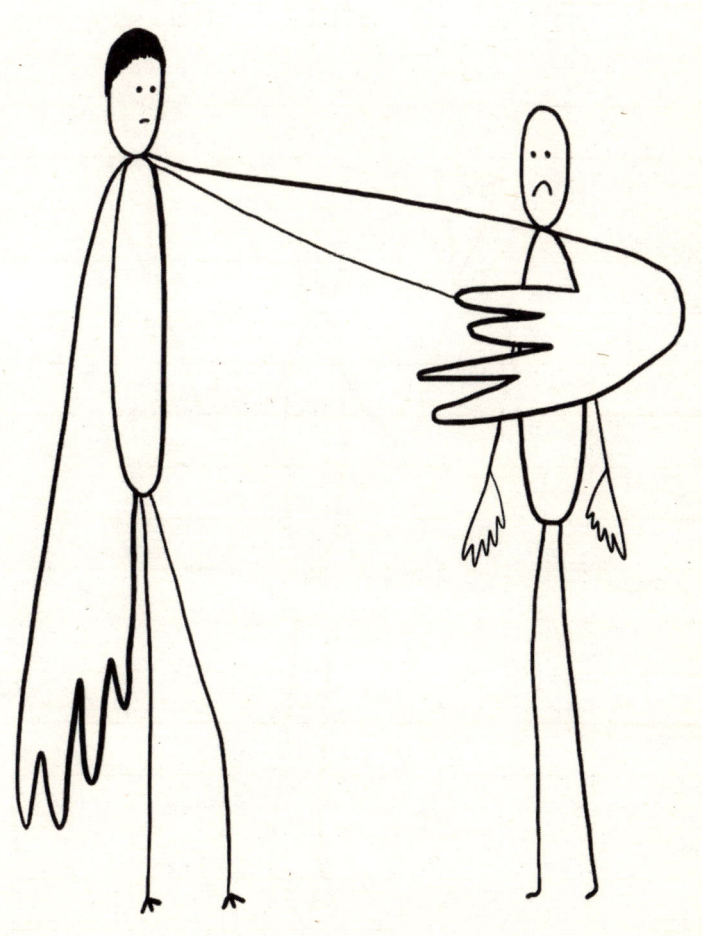

Because guess what?

You're still here.

Punch the dot if
you feel alive.

Side note:

The world's
happiest country
is Finland.

So if you want a
shortcut out of
your bad mood,
maybe just move
there.

Okay, so we've ascertained that your bad mood is a cake with a fried egg on top.

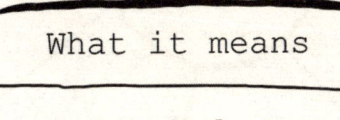

What it means

Preverbal angst

Fear of death

Hovering above your bad mood egg cake are your expectations that you should be in a better mood.

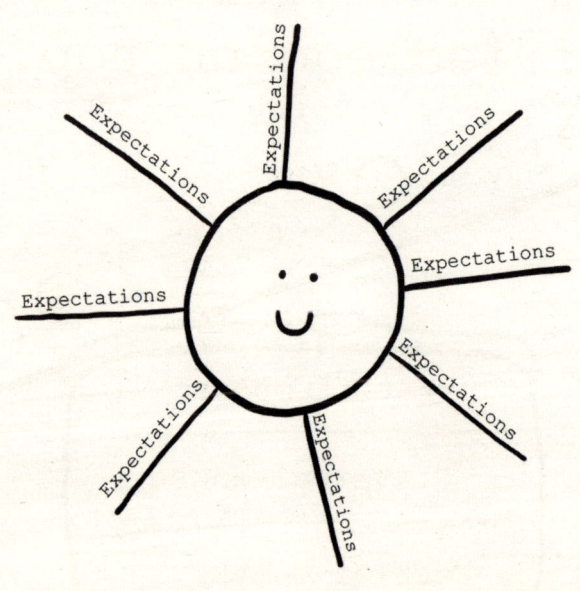

From afar, these expectations seem well-intentioned.

But they are not.

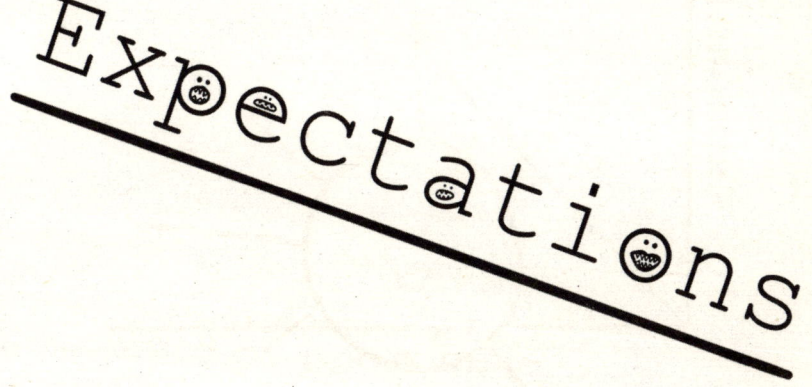

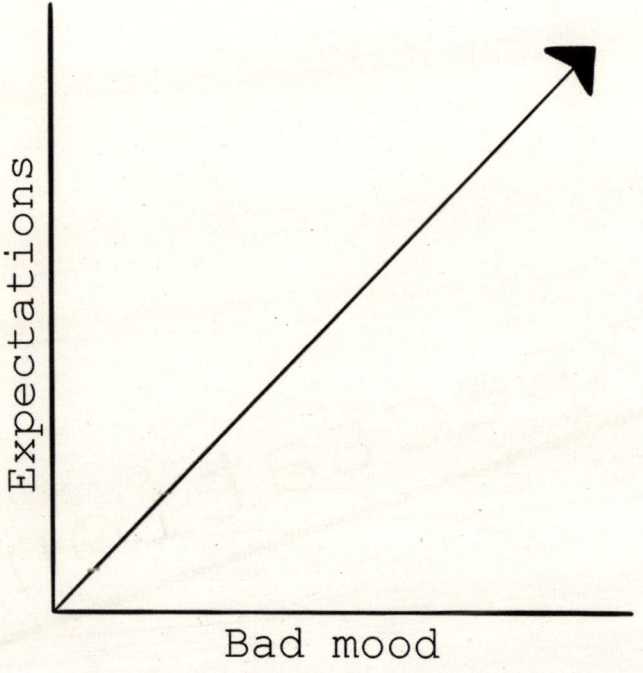

The more intense your
expectations are, the
crappier you'll feel.

How do you expect yourself to feel
right now?

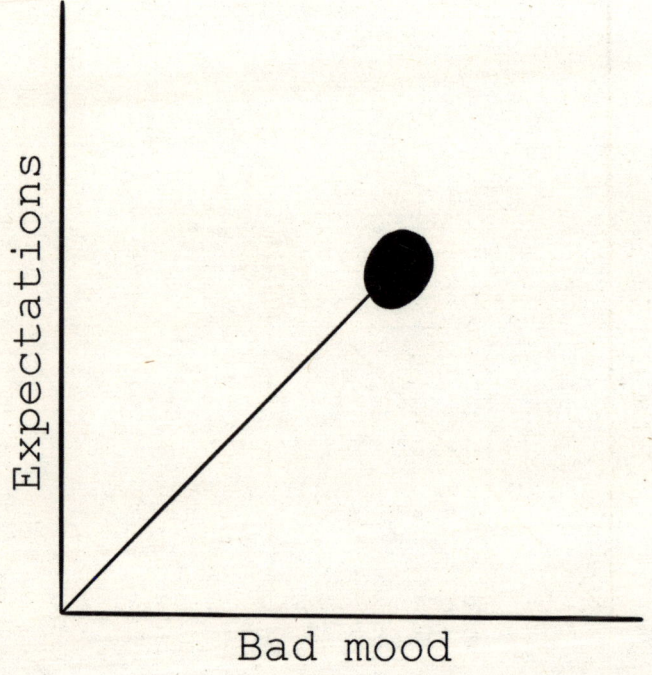

Please punch the
dot again.

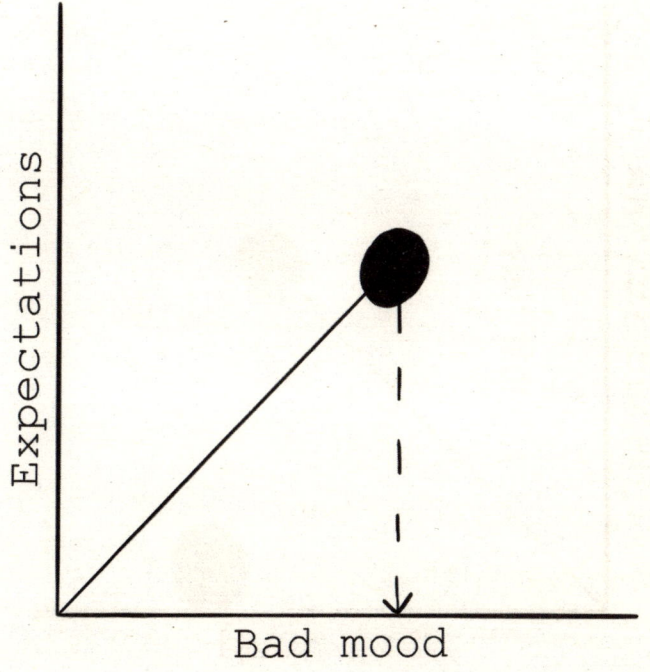

See how it's
falling?

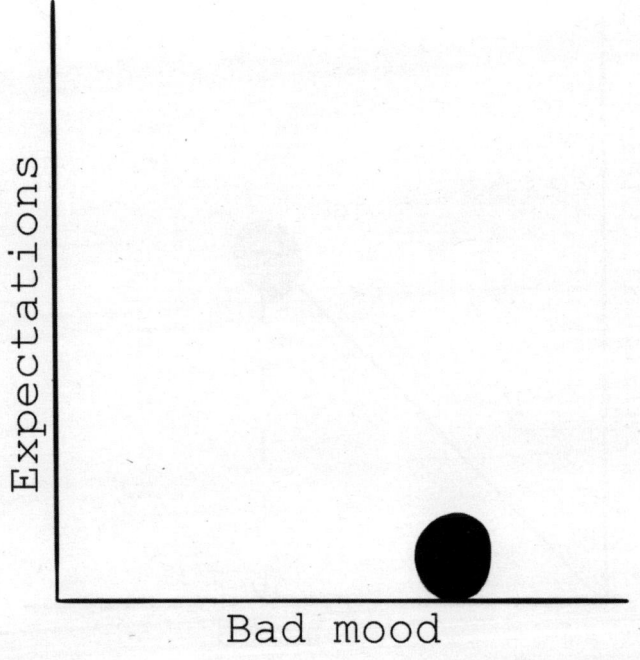

The dot now has no expectations.

Please imagine that you're the
expectation-less dot. How do you feel
now?

Realistically,
we're going to
have to do that
exercise over and
over because
expectations are
like freeway
flowers:
they never seem
to die.

Okay wait.

I have a surprise
for you.

They're on the
next page.

After a moment of
admiration, please
tear them out.

FREEWAY
FLOWERS

Sweet.

Moving forward, please
tear out every flower
you see in this book.

At some point, you're
probably going to tear
out some words along
with your flowers.

And that's okay.

Most things don't
matter that much,
including ripped
paper.

That seemed
important so
let's repeat
it.

Most things
don't matter
that much.

If you could remember this
all the time, you'd be in a
much better mood.

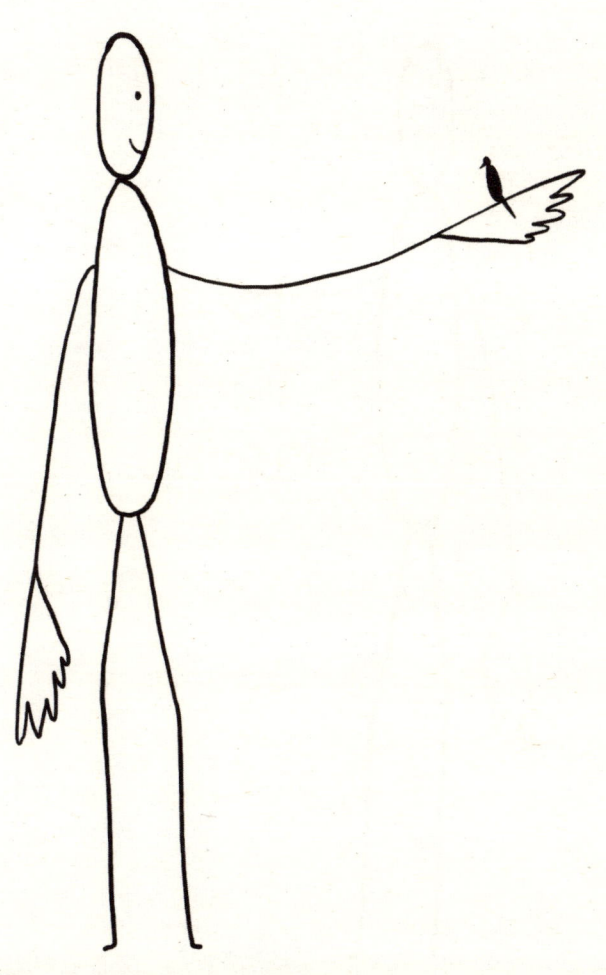

But you won't remember it
all the time.

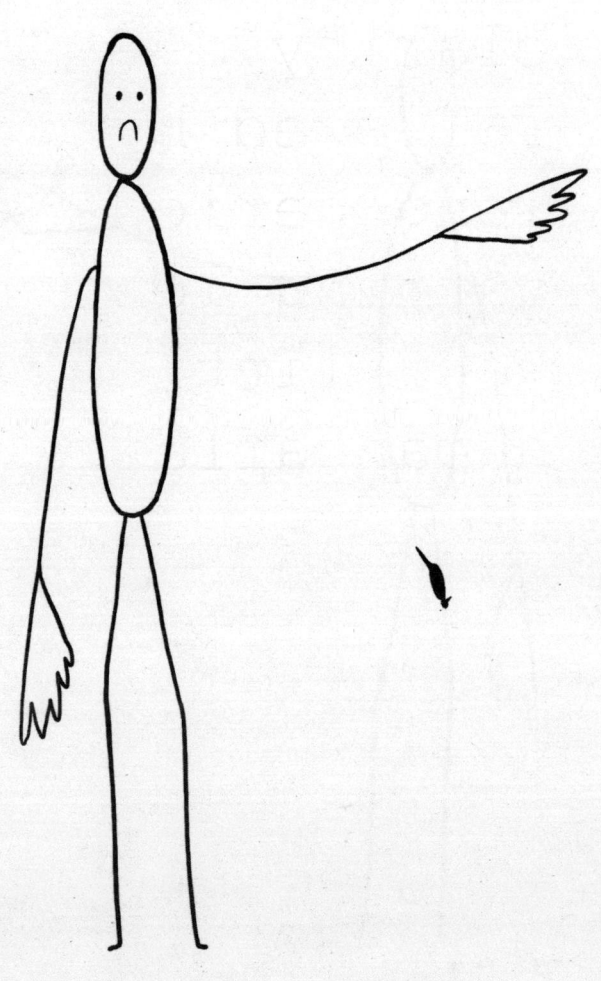

You'll have
moments of
clarity
followed by
long periods of
getting lost in
your little
human affairs.

You know how ants are
always running around
frantically trying to
gather materials?

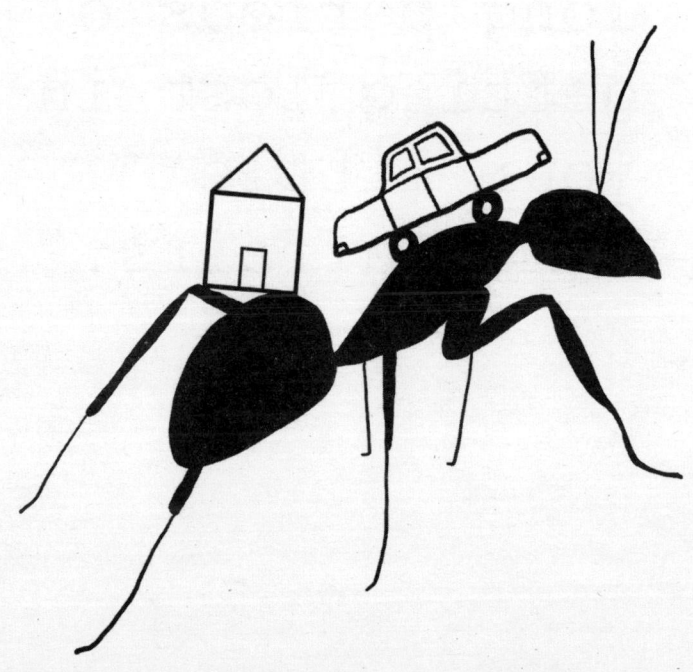

Have you ever
seen an ant who
is not stressed
about their
little ant
affairs?

If you've made any statements like this lately...

The lack of earth tones at Home Depot ruined my day.

The poorly wrapped burrito ruined my day.

The collarless shirt from Fred Segal got stained by a tomato, which ruined my day.

...then you have lost the plot.

Have you made any statements like this lately? If so, what were they? (Please try not to lie.)

Whatever dumb
stuff you've said
is okay.

Actually, it's
only natural.

We might live in
a modern world,
but our hard
drives are from
the Stone Age.

In other words, now that we're not running away from bears anymore, we're making tomato stains into bears.

As a side note, I recommend *pretending* to run away from a bear whenever you have some free time.

Exercise tells your inner cave person that you've survived something and you can chill now.

Please draw yourself in a good mood
even if you suck at drawing.

Please draw yourself in a bad mood.

Please draw yourself in your current mood.

Has your mood
changed since you
started this
book?

☐ Yes
☐ No
☐ Fuck off

If you answered
"no" or "fuck
off," please
scream at the dot,
then punch the
dot, then scribble
the dot out.

•

Now

(and this is for everyone)

chuck

this book

across the

room.

Seriously, just do it.

dot dot dot

Welcome back.

How was your retrieval
walk?

Did you feel like you
were playing fetch
with yourself?

I knew you needed a
break, and I wanted to
make it fun.

You're welcome.

Now
let's
consider
bad
moods
on
a
larger
scale.

We might think
bad moods begin
and end with us.

But this is
usually not how
it goes.

Most bad moods
have a ripple
effect.

If you're in a bad mood,
then you're more likely to
be mean to other people,
and this will likely put
them in a bad mood.

Also, after you're mean,
you'll feel remorse, which
will put you in a double bad
mood, and then you'll be even
more likely to be mean, and
this keeps going...

See how bad moods
cause more bad moods?

It's kind of like when
you see one stressed
out ant walking
alone...

...and then they stroll into their colony and stress out all the other ants.

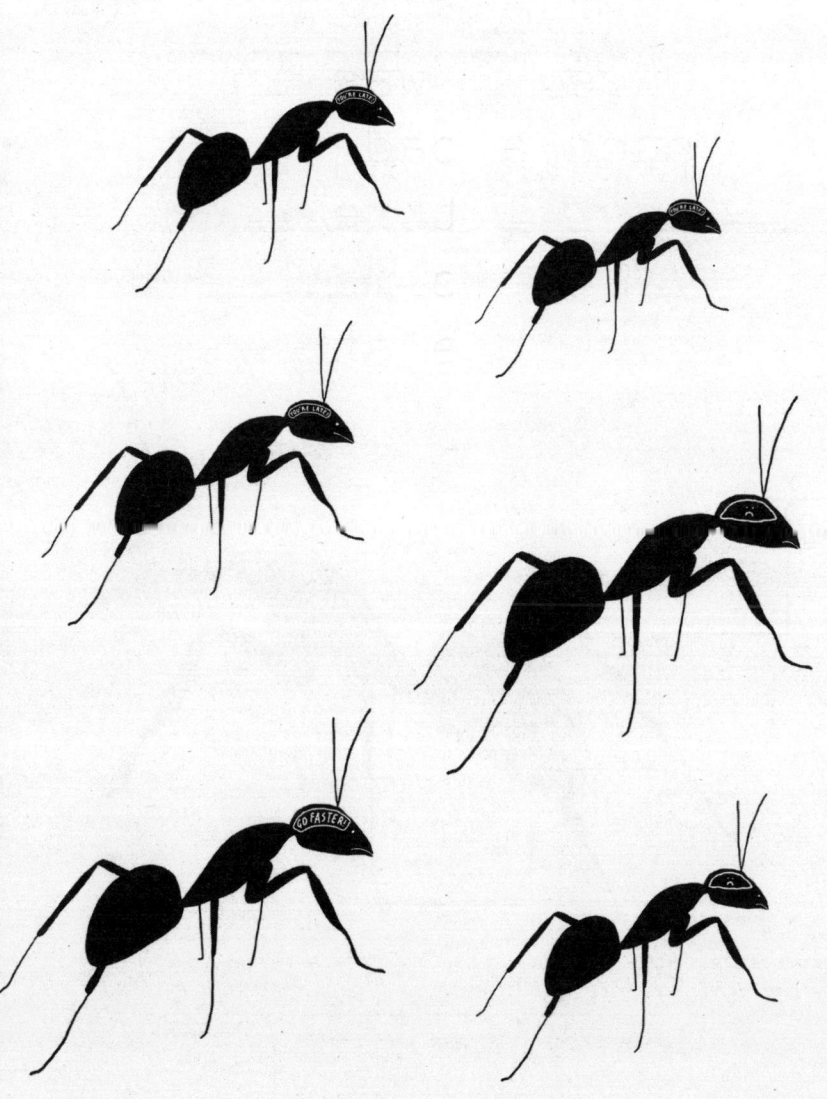

Once, I was in
such a bad mood
that I threw a
magnetic marble
down the stairs—

—and it hit a sliding glass
door.

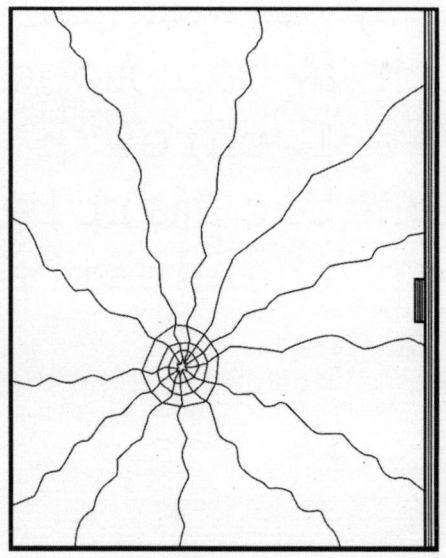

Cracks spider-webbed out from
the initial spot of impact,
and even though the sound was
weirdly soothing (ice cubes
clinking), I was already in a
double bad mood, because it
was my fault that we'd lost a
door.

Please write about a time when your
bad mood expanded into more badness.

When the people around you are in a bad mood, what's that like for you?

Another problem with
bad moods is that
they separate us
from a sense of
wonder.

Once, after a breakup, I was looking at this flower but all I could see was I HOPE YOU SLIP ON A BANANA PEEL AND DIE, BITCH!

What color was
that flower?

I have no idea
because I
couldn't see
it beyond my
rage.

Bad moods also
separate us from
other people.

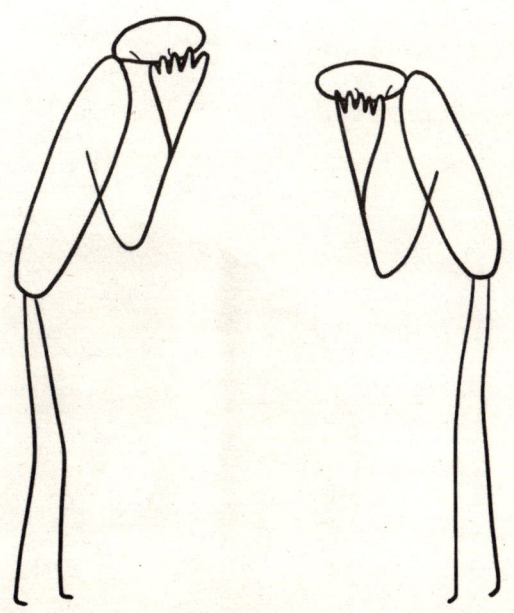

When we're in a
bad mood, we
often think we're
the only ones on
earth who feel
bummed and this
makes us feel
lonely.

Let's pretend we just shot
into the atmosphere and now
we're gazing down at our
city.

See how all the
buildings are
frowning?

That's because the
people inside of them
are also frowning.

Now let's do
something that is
going to involve
some thought:

Please imagine
loneliness as a
sound.

Would the sound be
loud enough

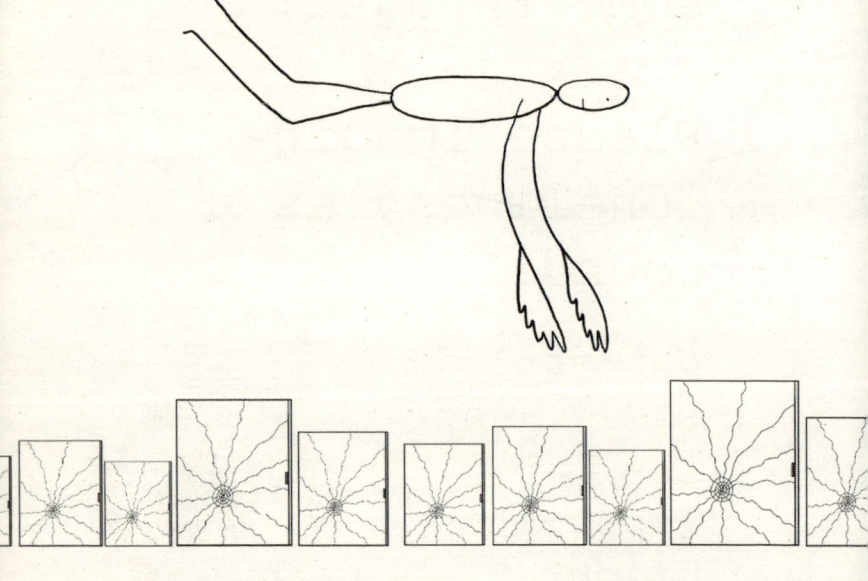

to shatter all the
sliding glass doors in
the city?

Now let's shoot into
outer space.

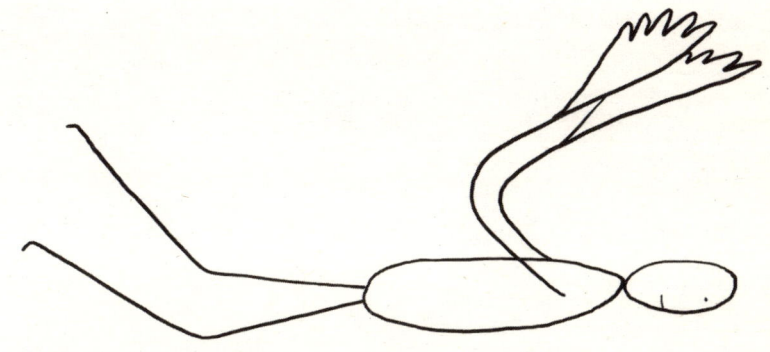

Can you
still hear
the
loneliness
of our
world from
here?

Do you know people who are in a bad mood right now? If so, what's going on with them?

When people you know are in a bad mood,
do you give them advice? If so, what is
it?*

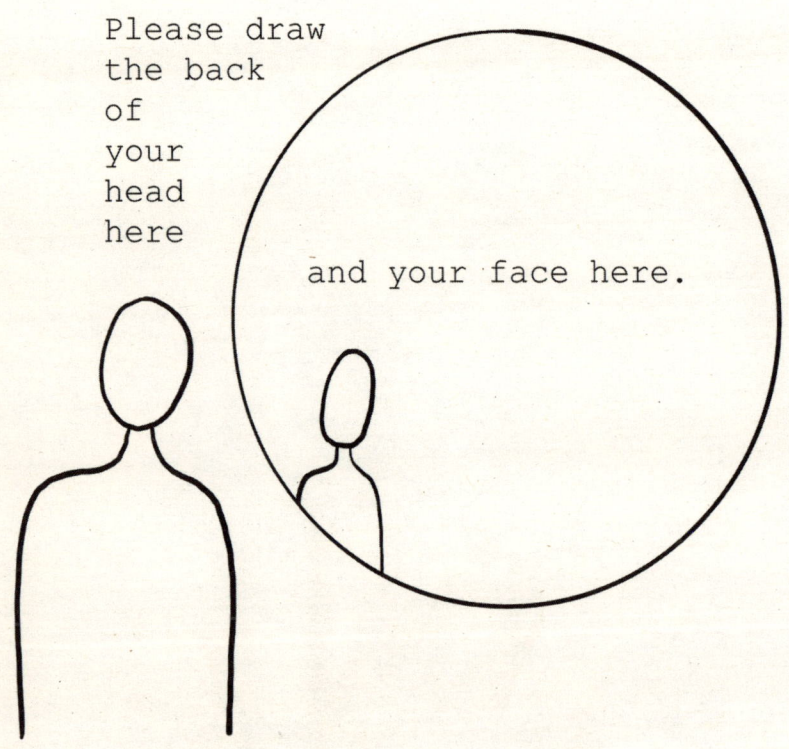

Please draw
the back
of
your
head
here

and your face here.

*I've found that the advice we
give is usually the advice we
need to take.

There are so many funny
things about humans.

For instance, even though we
know we're human, we still
think we can be robots.

I'm fine.
I'm fine.
I'm fine.

What is also
funny is how we
forget history.

Ideally, what percentage of
the time would you like to
spend in a good mood?

Please indicate your
preference on the pie chart
below using this key:

☐ Bad mood
■ Good mood

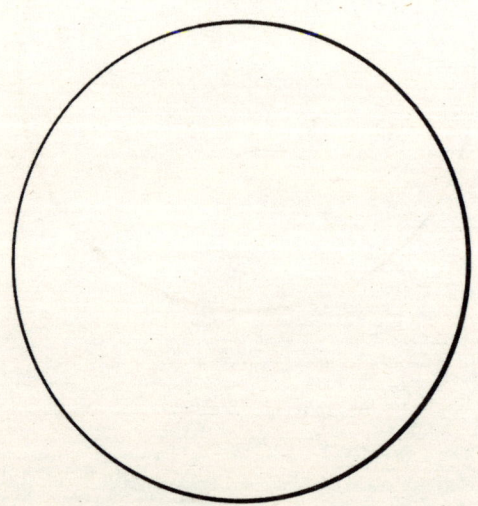

Historically, what
percentage of the time
have you spent in a
good mood?

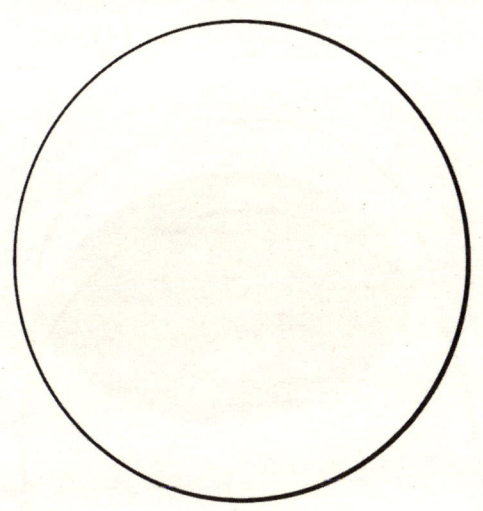

If your Ideal Pie Chart and
your Historical Pie Chart
don't look like twins, then
good morning! It's time to
wake up!

Here, I made you a coffee.

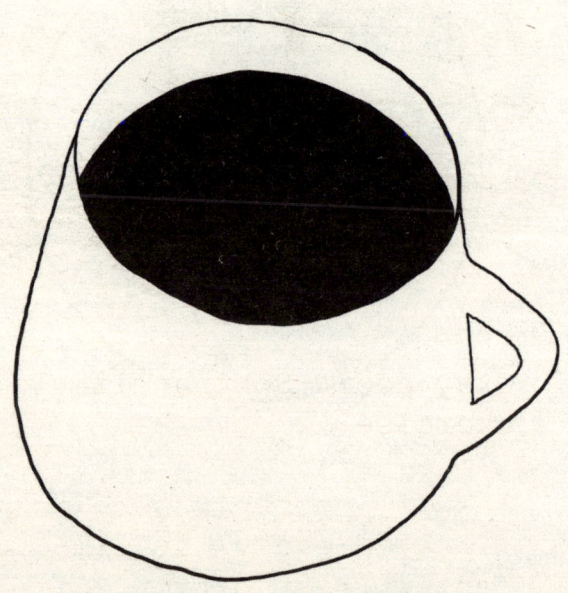

Remember how I said that
expectations, like freeway
flowers, never seem to die?

As you drink your coffee,
think about killing off your
expectations again.

Okay cool. So that little
exercise?

It will probably need to be
repeated every five minutes
for the rest of your life.

Now let's consider the past in
more detail.

How did you feel...

yesterday?

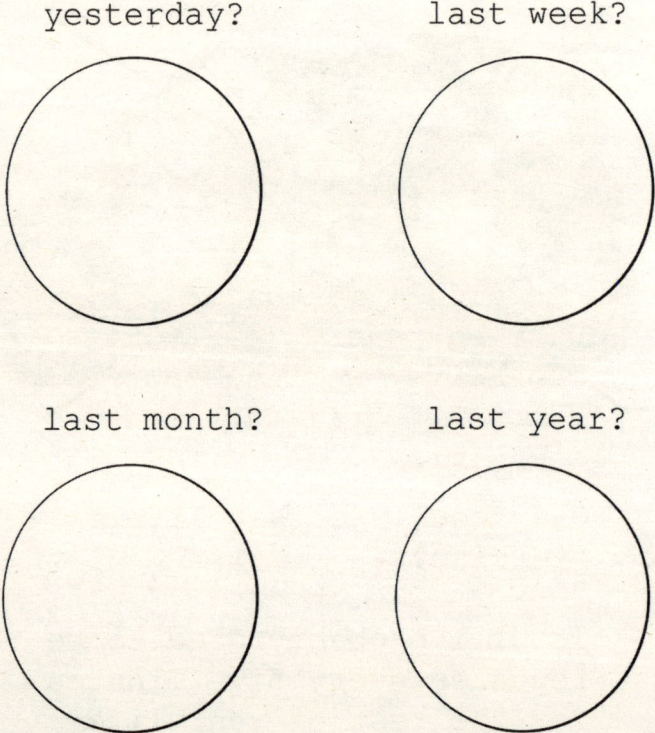

last week?

last month?

last year?

I'm wondering:

Do all the pie charts on the previous page look kind of similar?

If you're like, "No, my pie charts aren't similar at all because yesterday my cat died so I was in a bad mood and last week I won a car in a raffle so I was in a good mood..."

then please make a Mood Pie Chart for every year you've been alive, working backwards from now, until they start to look similar.

dot dot dot

Sweet. Now please fill in
this pie chart with your
average mood ratio:

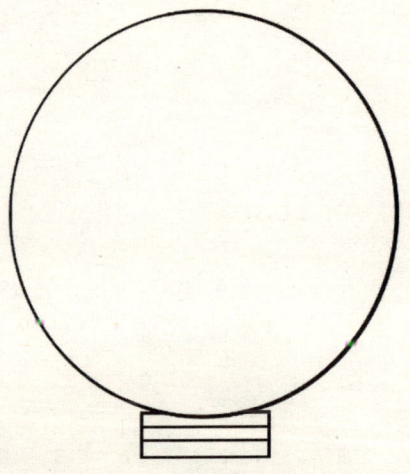

And peer into it.

Do you see your future?

This is your crystal ball.

Am I saying that given the past, you probably have the expertise to estimate the future?

Yes.

Am I saying that history repeats itself?

Mostly.

Am I saying that a bad mood is less about circumstance and more about how you deal with it?

Yes.

Of course, sometimes life throws tremendously dark things at us and the only reasonable response is to fall into the Bad Mood Hole.

And that's okay.

The question is: How long should we stay in there?

Let's solve this riddle by pinpointing the extremes.

On one side of the spectrum, we have the people who leap over every Bad Mood Hole and never stop smiling.

This is called toxic positivity.

I cannot fucking stand these people.

From afar, they look shiny.

But if you get close to them, you might notice that when you look away, they sigh.

And when you look back at them, they smile again.

I'll state the obvious here: ignoring your feelings doesn't work.

On the far other side of the
spectrum are the people who
gratefully belly flop into
every Bad Mood Hole and start
decorating the walls.

These people call everyone
who's still taking their
calls and say, "I barely
stubbed my toe and now I
can't get up! Help me!"

(Translation: "I feel most
like myself when I pretend to
have no agency.")

If this is you, take down
your decor, dude.

Wallowing doesn't work
either.

Here is the
answer to how
long you should
stay in your Bad
Mood Hole:

For as much time
as you need and
as little time as
possible.

What are your immediate habitual reactions to an oncoming bad mood? Do you call someone? Meditate? Eat fourteen sandwiches?

If you didn't love your answer to that last question, don't worry.

The cool thing about change is that once in a while it actually happens.

I'm now going to give you a
pair of glasses.

On one lens, please write
KIND and on the other lens
please write NESS.

Let's imagine that these are
two-way glasses. When you put
them on, you see yourself
with kindness and you see the
world with kindness.

I'm going to make the
argument that most
bad moods arise from
a lack of kindness,
and all of them
persist for the same
reason.

I think it often goes
like this: the world
is unkind to us, and
then we are unkind to
ourselves.

If the voice
in your head
is saying, "Be
happier,
asshole," your
bad mood will
last longer.

If the voice
says, "Oh
sweetheart," and
the hand that is
your hand covers
your heart, and
the breath that
is your breath
stops trying so
hard, your bad
mood is much less
likely to
persist.

A lot of people are like, "Your reality is dictated by what you think, so if your reality sucks, then change your thinking."

And I'm like, "Can we be more specific here? What should we be thinking about?"

We should
be thinking
about
kindness.

You can either be
kind because
you're evolved
and virtuous, or
you can do it for
this selfish
reason:

Being kind will
keep you out of
the Bad Mood
Hole.

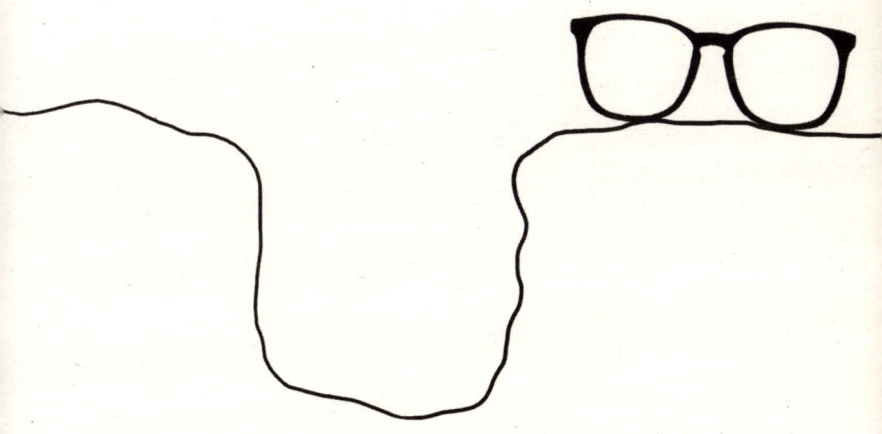

What are some kind things you did last week?

What are some kind things you're going
to do next week?

Perhaps the
funniest thing
about humans is
how complex we
think we are.

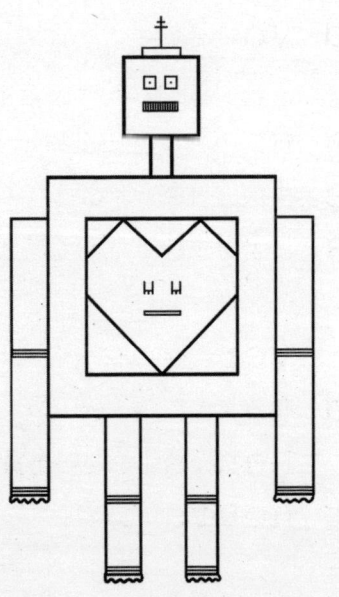

I'm complex.
I'm complex.
I'm complex.

Some questions:

Has eating when you're
hungry ever felt like
a downgrade?

Has playing with a
bouncy ball ever
depressed you?

Has being near the
ocean ever made you
feel less alive?

Have you ever
regretted taking a
bath and then sleeping
for eight hours?

The truth is that
our needs...

Food
Sleep
Exercise
Nature
Bouncy balls

...are the same
needs of dogs and
small children.

Remember when you
played fetch with
this book?

I was priming you
for the dog
comparison.

You're welcome.

Pretend that you
are your own dog.

Do you need to feed
yourself?

Take yourself for a
walk?

Sleep?

If there's anything
your dog self
needs, please go
take care of it.

Before we
move on,
let's
double
down.

I would like you to take a metaphorical final ice bath in your bad mood.

Here's how to do that:

With as much
drama and
extravagance
as you can
fathom...

Sink deeper into your bad
mood.

Roll around in your bad mood.

Bathe in your bad mood.

Swaddle yourself in your bad
mood.

Stare at your bad mood.

Apply your bad mood all over
your body like lotion.

Eat your bad mood.

Embrace your bad mood.

Embrace it tighter.

And tighter.

And tighter than
that.

And whisper,
"See you next
time."

NOW
FLY
UP AND
OUT
OF YOUR
BAD MOOD
HOLE.

Not sure if you noticed, but
your hands have been growing
into wings this whole time.

Draw your beautiful face sleeping.
Fill up the entire page.

See how peaceful
you look?

Now tear that
drawing out.

And gather all
your flowers.

Place all but one
of them around
your beautiful
sleeping face.

Is this a
celebration of
self-love or is
it a nod to your
funeral?

Let's say that
it's both.

Let's say you can forget everything in this book except for these two things:

1. You are going to die one day.

2. So while you're still here, be about 400 notches kinder to yourself than you think you need to be.

If you start
there, it will be
a lot easier to
be 400 notches
kinder than you
think you need to
be to everyone
else.

It's easy to look around and be like, "Other people know what they're doing and I do not."

This is especially true when those other people are wearing good clothes.

I promise you
that nobody knows
what they're
doing.

I also promise
you that the
people who tell
you they know
what they're
doing are more
lost than the
rest of us.

We are all just rushing
around frantically
gathering materials.

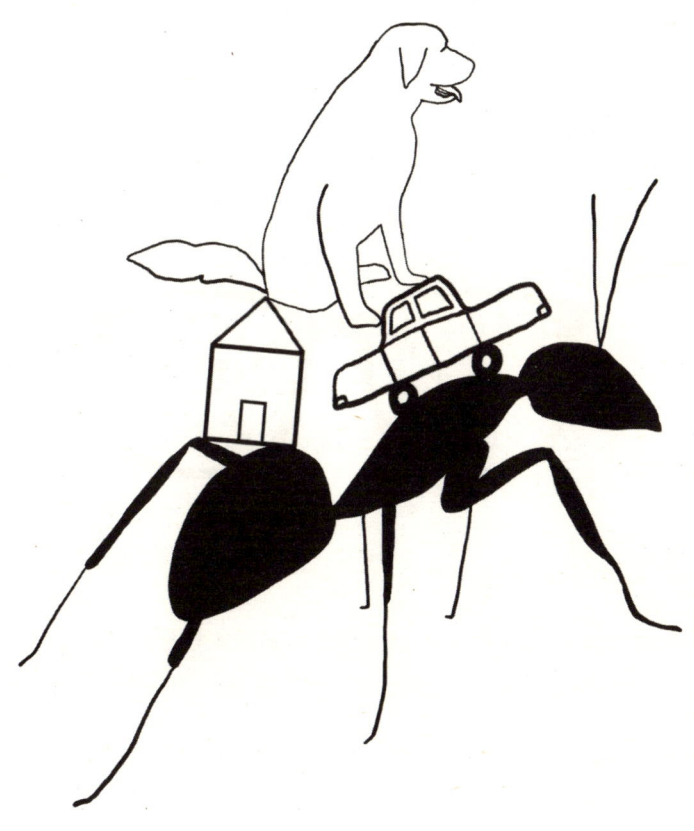

We are all losing
the plot multiple
times a day.

We are all confused babies who
happen to be old now.

We are all
forgetting to
imagine
loneliness as
a sound.

You have one flower
left.

Please give it to
someone who's in a bad
mood right now.

If it seems
appropriate, maybe you
can put your arm
around them

and say...

I'm sorry you're
in a bad mood.

Want to rip up
some paper?

This book
only exists because:

1. My mom gave me her old iPad,

2. Nicole Tourtelot said, "You should write a gift book" on a hike one day,

3. Nora Gonzalez (so smart and kind) sold the book, and

4. Lauren Appleton (who has a wonderfully dry sense of humor) bought it.

5. Also, Fletcher, you're my formatting genius;

6. Bolt, you're my forever-rock; and

7. Fig, you're my favorite sounding board because you have good taste and don't lie.

To people 1-7, thank you.